U·S·A·F
TODAY

U•S•A•F
TODAY

Walter Wright

OSPREY
AEROSPACE

Dedicated to Alice Price, with many thanks for all her help

Published in 1992 by Osprey Publishing Limited, 59 Grosvenor Street, London W1X 9DA

© Walter Wright

ISBN 1 85532 223 4

Editor Tony Holmes
Page design by Paul Kine
Printed in Hong Kong

Title page Heading for the stratosphere a 'Jersey Devil' of the 177th Fighter Interceptor Group pulls into the vertical during a simulated dogfight. The F100 engine develops 18,000 lbs of thrust (equal to the F-16's empty weight), allowing a partially loaded aircraft to climb dramatically

Front cover Now tasked with the demanding close-air support (CAS) role, the F/A-16s of the 138th Tactical Fighter Squadron (TFS) rarely get to cruise at this altitude, performing their 'FAST ASS/CAS' missions at ultra low-level. Currently equipped with the only F/A-16s in the 'Guard, the 'Boys from Syracuse' will eventually be joined by several other units in this 'gunfighter' role as more A-7D Corsair IIs are retired

Back cover 'Gently does it.' With the most visible air-to-air refuelling receptacle of any USAF aircraft in service today, the B-1B is a 'dream machine' for pilots when it comes to the tricky procedure of in-flight tanking. All the aircrew have to do is lean forward slightly, take a peek over the instrument coaming and guide the 'flying boom' into the receptacle

For a catalogue of all books published by Osprey Aerospace please write to:

The Marketing Department, Octopus Illustrated Books, 1st Floor, Michelin House, 81 Fulham Road, London SW3 6RB

Above A-10 squadron commander's aircraft 'Panther One' of the 353rd TFS photographed at RAF Bentwaters, a long way from its home base at Myrtle Beach in South Carolina. The only external store is a travel pod on the fuselage centreline

Introduction

Global Reach – Global Power. Words that describe the United States Air Force of the 1990s. A concept proven during the Gulf War in 1991. The Air Force aircraft which provide an awesome combat capacity are lavishly depicted in this volume. They are flown, supported, and maintained by a unique 'Total Force' resourced from both active and reserve components.

Regardless of component, the United States Air Force trains to one standard of excellence. Pilots from Active Duty Units, the Air National Guard and the Air Force Reserve often fly the same type of aircraft and always meet the same demanding standards. A carefully balanced force structure has addressed issues of affordability and accessability, providing 'hybrid vigour' for the force. Each component contributes according to its particular advantage and the Air Force gains strength from the diversity.

The Gulf War provided a full view of the strength of our Air Force in action. Active and volunteer Reserve Forces responded immediately to the invasion of Kuwait. Aerial bridges provided immediate combat power and contained Iraqi forces. Airpower sustained a rapid force build-up and provided flexible options. The activation of Reserve Force combat units sent a final diplomatic signal of resolve. Those same units were flying some of the toughest missions of the war less than two weeks later.

Airpower seized the initiative with a carefully planned attack which first paralysed the Iraqi Command and Control, then shaped the battlefield for the invasion which liberated Kuwait.

There was only one United States Air Force in the Central Command. No Guardsmen, no Tactical Air Command pilots, no Air Force Reservists; just one force fighting effectively under CENTAF Command. That's what makes the United States Air Force the best in the world!

I hope you enjoy the photographs of the special people and aircraft which make it happen.

Brigadier General Mike Hall,
Commanding Officer 174th Tactical Fighter Wing.

Right 'Baton 01' (the EC-130 call sign) of the 193rd Special Operations Group holds positon just off the boom of 'Shake 81' (a KC-135E of the 171st ARefw) while 'Sandy 21' (an OA-10 of the 111th Tactical Air Support Group) rides off the left wing. Although hardly evident in this shot, the dark grey KC-135 camouflage uses the same grey as the OA-10, which is the same grey seen in the strategic camouflage scheme

Contents

The 'Rhino'

The Air National Guard, a development of the 18th-century state militias, was created in 1946. ANG squadron, group, and wing designations are generally numbered between 101 and 199 (with a few recent units forming in the 200s). The first Phantom IIs to go to the 'Guard arrived in 1971 when RF-4Cs were assigned to Alabama. RF-4Cs were the only Phantom IIs still assigned in late 1991, although 'Guard units had also flown F-4Cs, Ds, and Es, and are currently preparing to receive F-4G Advanced Wild Weasels.

One of the last Air Force units to fly the F-4E was the 141st Tactical Fighter Squadron (TFS) of the New Jersey Air National Guard's 108th Tactical Fighter Wing (TFW). The 141st's scheduled transition to F-16s was postponed in 1989, and eventually cancelled. In late 1991 the squadron had relinquished the last of their Phantom IIs and converted to KC-135s. The aircrew of this Phantom II rest on a practice missile whilst completing their pre-flight inspection

Above Photographer Walter Wright looking suitably pleased with himself following a mission in an F-4E of the New Jersey Air National Guard

Left The 141st Aero Squadron fought in France during World War 1, adopting as its emblem a Tiger mauling a German spiked helmet. At McGuire AFB in the 1980s the 141st TFS resurrected this old insignia, took the nickname 'Jersey Tigers', and began stencilling tiger faces on its aircraft. This photo shows three versions of the tiger face: tan stencil on European One camouflage, grey stencil on Hill Grey camouflage, and shaded grey on Hill Grey camouflage

Above Waiting at 'Last Chance'. Here final inspections are performed, weapons and ejection seats are armed, and the flight is cleared to taxy for take-off

Above right En route to the bombing range, two 'Jersey Tiger' Phantom IIs climb to altitude. At this height the European One scheme darkens dramatically

Right A closer view of the flight leader reveals small blue BDU-33 practice bombs on a TER (triple-ejector rack) beneath the wing. Note how the light shows through the rudder counter balance

Brigadier General Robert Applegate, 108th TFW commander, banks his F-4E away from the camera. Underwing stores include a Pave Spike laser designator in the forward left missile trough, an empty TER under the right wing, and a 600-gallon fuel tank on the centreline

Above Unlike most other National Guard organizations, the DC-ANG, based at Andrews AFB, Maryland, reports to the Secretary of the Army (most Guard units report to their respective state governors; the District of Columbia is not a state). The DC-ANG's 121st TFS, 113th TFW, flew F-4Ds until their conversion to F-16s in 1990. Here, ground crews pre-flight a European One camouflaged Phantom II for a winter mission

Right Looking at a Phantom II you see proof of the maxim that 'you can make a brick fly, if you give it a big enough engine'. Here, just before take-off those powerful General Electric engines are warming up and in a moment the backseater will burrow deeper into his seat. A quick scan of the gauges as you stand hard on the brakes and run them up to 80 per cent. Their scream becomes deafening while you punch the throttle, let it off, and punch it again and hold it wide open with the afterburner adding its own wail as you release the brakes and erupt down the runway. Now the thumps of the expansion joints are hitting your seat bottom like a burst of machine gun fire; at about 165 knots the thumps virtually disappear as aerodynamic lift has taken the load off your tyres and suspension. At 176 it will fly, but to allow a safety margin you keep the nose down while adding a few more knots; at 185 or so (or a bit more if you have a long runway) you pull back on the stick and the ugly duckling becomes a swan

Above 'Brave 12' (the domestic call sign, drawn from the Washington Redskins football team) tucks in behind 'Brave 11's' right wing. In this view the 121st TFS insignia is clearly visible behind the intake

Above right Moving to the left, 'Brave 12' poses over the Chesapeake Bay. The tail stripe and stars originated in George Washington's family coat of arms. The one-two-one spacing of the stars is for the 121st TFS

Right Banking for home, 'Brave 12' displays the two-toned undersides of its Hill Grey two camouflage scheme. Even at this close range the pattern mimics that on the upper surfaces

Above The New York ANG's 136th Figher Interceptor Squadron (FIS)/107th Fighter Interceptor Group (FIG), flew F-4Ds for air defence of the US and Canada. The 136th is based at Niagara Falls International Airport, the blue and green tail markings representing the famous falls

Right Symbolic of mass and power, the F-4 is called 'Rhino' by its crews. The 136th added the rhinoceros silhouette to its Phantom IIs in the late 1980s. The grey bars below the cockpit are a low-vis presentation of the Distinguished Unit Citation; the oak leaf notes that the award was earned twice and the 'V' (for valour) denotes a third award in combat. The maple leaf is a zap added by Canadian crews during a visit to a Canadian base

Falcons

The 119th FIS, 177th FIG ('Jersey Devils') fly air defence missions in late-model F-16As from Atlantic City, New Jersey. Returning from a deployment, these aircraft each carry a 300-gallon centreline tank and two 370-gallon wing tanks

Above A right side portrait from a two-seat F-16B. As is standard practice with ANG F-16 units, the 119th FIS operates a single 'twin stick' Bravo model primarily to provide check rides for new aircrew assigned to the squadron

Left The view from the refuelling station of a KC-135. Most F-16s carry low-visibility grey unit markings, but each unit will use colour to identify one aircraft as the commander's. Compare the clarity of the red markings on the second aircraft with the similar grey markings on the aircraft in the foreground

Above Many Guard units are based at civil airports. Headquarters for the 177th FIG is a secure area at Atlantic City International Airport

Left A 177th F-16 banks to starboard. A single Sidewinder is carried on the wingtip rail, the practice missile's infrared sensors enabling the aircraft to track targets during combat training

Above Much of the Atlantic coast is recreational, with the beaches of New Jersey being among the best. The sun glints off the water as the aircraft heads for an off-shore dogfight with the camera ship

Right The wing root of the F-16 is blended into the fuselage, the compression of the airflow in this area creating contrails under many atmospheric conditions

Above A belly shot, as the F-16 rolls near the top of a loop. The Atlantic whitecaps below offer little visual impression of altitude

Left Atlantic City, with its casinos and boardwalk, forms an impressive backdrop as a 119th F-16 heads north along the coast. The 'Jersey Devils' are one of nine ANG units tasked with fighter interceptor duties, being equipped with suitably converted Block 15 Air Defense Fighter (ADF) Fighting Falcons

Above left What the 1990s F-16 pilot wears. Helmet in bag, Capt. Pete Nyce, 121st TFS, returns from a practice mission. The G-suit around his waist and legs prevents blackouts during hard turns. Straps in the cockpit attach his harness to the seat-mounted parachute and survival kit. A 'poopy suit' (or exposure suit, seen at his neck and right wrist) is worn under his flight suit as a precaution during overwater flights

Above right 'The Boys from Syracuse' operate their F/A-16s primarily in the ground attack and Close Air Support (CAS) missions, the 138th TFS/174th TFW being the first unit assigned this radical new role for the Fighting Falcon. Nicknamed 'Fastass CAS', the 138th TFS have modified their F-16s to carry a GPU-5/A 'Pave Claw' 30 mm gun pod on the centreline station in place of the almost mandatory external tank

Left A gut-wrenching turn – the F-16 can turn harder than its pilots. And at only five Gs, a camera, motor drive and lens can weigh 30 lbs!

Above The 174th TFW carries a Fighting Falcon silhouette on the right side of the aircraft, with a cobra silhouette on the left

Right Heading for a gap in the clouds, two 'Boys' indulge in a spot of 'follow-my-leader' as they emerge from a loop and rapidly close on the Atlantic thousands of feet below

Above Although the F/A-16 performed well in the 1990 *Gunsmoke* exercise, achieving second place overall, in the crucible of combat during *Desert Storm* computer software interface problems between the gun and the aircraft's avionics restricted the unit to only a single day's action over Kuwait

Right Two F-16s from 136th FIS after conversion from F-4Ds. The bulge at the base of the vertical tail is characteristic of F-16s which have been modified for air defence. The cataract of Niagara Falls is now represented with two parallel grey bands

Above The same aircraft in 'finger-four' formation; the camouflages are similar, though the Syracuse aircraft show more fading than the recently repainted Niagara Falls aircraft. Note also the different camouflage demarcations around the cockpits

Right This Falcon formation shot shows the two types of horizontal tails carried on F-16/As and Bs. The narrower tail, seen on 'The Boys from Syracuse', was succeeded in later models by the 'big tail' seen on the Niagara Falls aircraft

Eagles

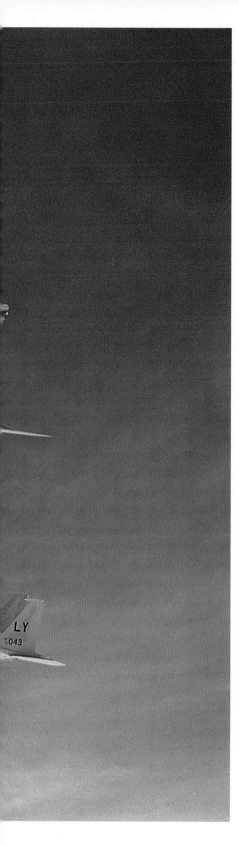

Left During the height of the Cold War, hundreds of regular USAF, ANG, and Air Force Reserve fighters were assigned to the air defence of North America. By the 1990s the number of aircraft had been reduced dramatically, and the mission had been concentrated in the Air National Guard. These F-15As are from the 48th FIS, the last regular air force unit assigned to North American air defence

Below The 48th's 'LY' tail codes come from the unit's home station, Langley AFB, Virginia. The Disney-designed cat emblem seen on the intake was first used by the 48th FS during World War 2 and readopted by the 48th FIS in 1988

Above The standard F-15 camouflage takes the form of two countershaded greys. While the pattern on the nose is not always apparent, this view offers a good comparison of the inner and outer tail surfaces. Although aircraft assigned to Pacific Air Forces (PACAF) wear the same pattern, the PACAF greys have more contrast

Right The 48th carries the insignia of the First Air Force on its right intake – the First Air Force moved from Langley to Tyndall AFB, Florida, in late 1991. The 48th FIS will be inactivated during 1992

An F-15A takes 8000 lbs of fuel from a KC-10 tanker. The lighting emphasizes the upper surface camouflage details. The Eagle has been dubbed the 'supersonic tennis court' by envious adversaries because of its huge wing area

Above Unlike other Eagles, F-15Es are camouflaged in a single dark grey shade overall. The squadron emblem on the intake and the yellow tail stripe mark the 336th TFS 'Rocketeers'. The 'SJ' (Seymour Johnson AFB) tail codes are now appropriate for 4th Wing KC-10s, too!

Left An F-15E of the 335th TFS/4th Wing. After returning from *Desert Storm* the three F-15E squadrons of the 4th TFW were joined by the two KC-10 squadrons of the deactivating 68th ARW (Air Refuelling Wing) to form the new 4th Wing. The 4th traces its history back to World War 2's 4th Fighter Group, formed from the RAF's three Eagle squadrons

Above Two 335th F-15Es break away from the tanker. In total, the squadron destroyed more than 400 tanks and artillery pieces in Kuwait and Iraq, mostly with laser guided ordnance

Left A second F-15E banks away after refuelling; the emblem and green tail band belong to the 335th TFS, nicknamed the 'Chiefs'. Along with the 336th TFS this squadron was heavily involved in the Gulf conflict, tallying over 5000 hours during the brief air war

Mud movers

The USAF's two slowest ground attack aircraft are the A-7 Corsair II and the A-10 Thunderbolt II. In the late 1980s wing cracks caused the Air Force to plan the retirement of all A-7s by 1993. The A-10 fared better, particularly after combat over Iraq, but current planning will still dramatically reduce the number of A-10s in service by 1993.

Left This 1991 series of photos of the 146th TFS/112th TFG was taken one month before the unit transitioned out of A-7Ds. The two-toned disruptive camouflage uses the same colours as the Hill Grey II F-4s. This close-up, taken from the unit's two-seat A-7K, shows the variety of markings possible in a unit even during peacetime. The nearest aircraft carries its radio call number in a newly approved position ahead of the refuelling receptacle, this A-7 also being the only one to display the outstanding unit award, whilst the far aircraft carries nose art aft of the cockpit

Above The right side of the same formation shows additional differences: the 'PT' (for Pittsburgh) tail codes appear in light grey, dark grey or black. Also, only three aircraft carry the 'Pennsylvania' tail band

Right The forests of Pennsylvania confirm that light greys aren't necessarily the best camouflage for ground attack!

Left Up close and personal – perfect placement and lighting sharpen the details for those who enjoy counting rivets

Overleaf Since 1946 the 146th TFS has flown only single-seat, single-engined fighters. In late 1991 the unit ended this association when it converted to KC-135s

Above Pennsylvania's 103rd Tactical Air Support Squadron (TASS), 111th TAS Group (TASG), based at Willow Grove, flies OA-10 Warthogs as forward air control aircraft. Several aircraft sported red keystones on their nacelles (strategically positioned in the middle of the 13 colonies, Pennsylvania became known as the Keystone State during the American Revolution). This example, with tail colours for the squadron's three flights, is assigned to the group commander

Right A dream to maintain, the A-10 opens quickly to allow access to all systems. This ease of access, combined with a simplicity of systems, has given the Warthog the best ratio of flying hours to maintenance hours of any USAF type

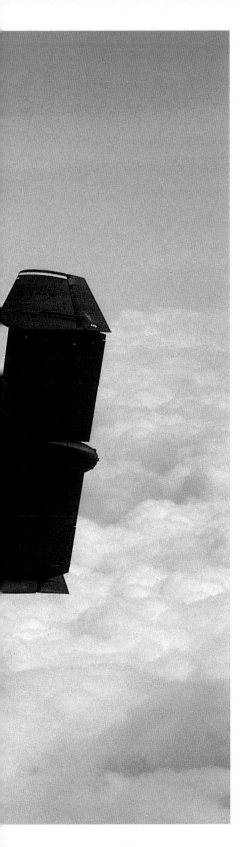

Above Standard markings for the 103rd TASS include 'PA' (for Pennsylvania) tail codes, flight-colour tail band (yellow for A-Flight), plane-in-squadron number at the base of the rudder, and the last three digits of the serial repeated on the wing tip

Left Banking for the camera. A-10s are not converted to OA-10s, they are simply reassigned to Forward Air Control duties. This 103rd TASS Warthog has been lightened by the removal of four bomb racks, a feature common to OA-10s and A-10s

Above The A-10's GAU-8 Avenger is the most powerful gun ever carried by an aircraft. The seven-barrel Gatling gun combines a high rate of fire (120 rounds in a two-second burst) with a heavy, spiked 30 mm round to devastate targets

Left At altitude, the A-10's three-colour camouflage invariably appears black against the clouds

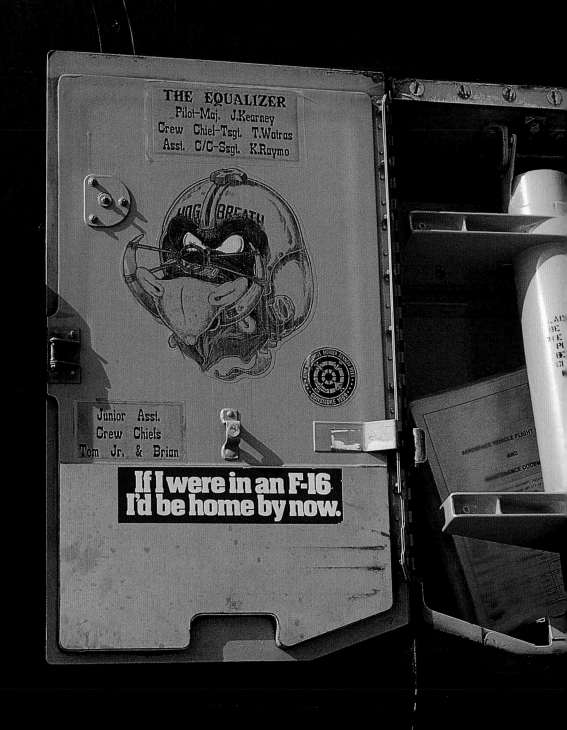

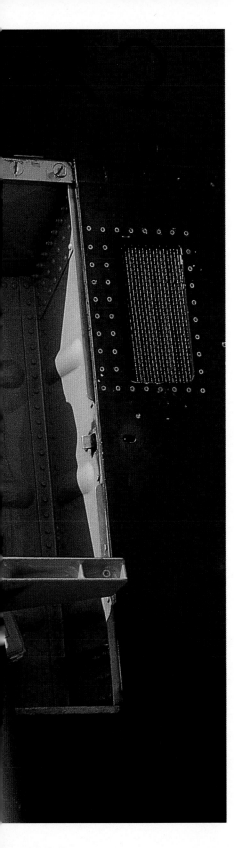

Above In a comparison of markings with the 103rd TASS, Connecticut's 118th TFS/103rd TFG leaves a drab impression. The dark grey 'CT' tail codes disappear, as does the stencilled group emblem on the nacelle

Left Many A-10 crews have overcome prohibitions on nose art by decorating the insides of boarding ladder doors. The result is called 'door art'! This Connecticut A-10 combines a drawing by aviation artist Hank Caruso with a soon-to-be-fulfilled wish for F-16s – the 118th TFS will complete conversion to F-16s in 1992

SAC

The origins of the Strategic Air Command (SAC) can be traced to a 1943 decision to allow the Eighth Air Force to concentrate on the long-range strategic bombing of Germany; the responsibility for a tactical campaign was moved to a reformed Ninth Air Force. SAC was created in 1947, developing into a force of intercontinental bombers and missiles, long-range reconnaissance aircraft, and supporting tankers. By the time of the Gulf War, mission distinctions had become blurred – SAC bombers flew only tactical missions, while tactical bombers and missiles were responsible for all strategic missions. In June 1992 SAC will be disbanded, with its assets divided between three commands; Air Combat Command, Air Mobility Command, and a unified Strategic Command.

Mohawk Warrior, a thirty-two-year-old B-52G (BMW) displays the new SAC gunship grey camouflage scheme. The 416th identified each bomber with a painting of the Statue of Liberty on the vertical tails, but the markings were removed during the war with Iraq

Above Markings on the *Mohawk Warrior*'s forward fuselage include personal artwork (marked during application of the new camouflage), mission markings from the Gulf War, a subdued presentation of the wing insignia, the last four digits of the aircraft serial number (57-6515), and a black silhouette of the state of New York

Right Members of the 416th BMW training high above the frozen landscape of Maine: a 668th BS B-52G refuels from a 509th ARS KC-135A. Note how fuel venting aft of the pilot's window follows the slipstream over the special leading edge fillets. By agreement with the Soviets, many cruise missile-equipped B-52s carried these fillets as a visual identification cue

Above *High Roller*, another 416th B-52G (58-0231), awaits maintenance on the Griffis hard stand. Two red bomb symbols record service in the Gulf War

Left Refuelling doors still open, the B-52 drops away from the tanker. Note that the covers for the chin-mounted electro-optical viewing system (EVS) have been retracted

Above A classic portrait of *Gunsmoke* (serial 85-0082), which displays a faded version of the strategic camouflage scheme applied to most SAC bombers during the 1980s. If compared with the colours on the similarly painted 416th B-52s, the olive drab seen here has been bleached to brown by the Texas sun

Right SAC operates four wings of B-1B Lancers for nuclear deterrence – crews are not cross-trained for the conventional 'iron bomb' missions that B-52s flew in the Gulf War. This aircraft hails from the 96th BMW, Dyess AFB, Texas

Above Captain Shaun Sorensen of the 528th BS/380th BMW begins the cockpit check prior to a training mission. The last of SAC's FB-111s retired a few months after this photo was taken

Left A second 96th B-1B approaches its tanker over the rugged mountains of New Mexico. Unfortunately the Lancer was about the only USAF frontline type not involved in the Gulf War, SAC's fleet being grounded at the time due to both structural and electronic problems

Above Although this FB-111A appears darker than the preceding B-52s and B-1Bs, it is painted in the same strategic camouflage scheme. A practice bomb dispenser hangs from the right outboard wing rack

Right and overleaf A pose for the camera, drop back, and roll away! With the same length as a World War 2 B-17 (and twice the gross weight), the FB-111 displays an agility that reflects its fighter origins. Note the reversing of the horizontal stabilizers. Regarded as the 'bastard child' in SAC ranks, only 76 of the planned 210 FB-111s eventually entered service, the remaining aircraft never being built due to a drastic shortage in funding. Because of their paucity in numbers, only two wings (the 380th and 509th) were ever equipped with the long-span FB-111A. Somewhat neglected by the SAC hierarchy over the years following their introduction to service in October 1969, the FB-111 fleet experienced little updating over the ensuing decades, resulting in the aircraft being far from 'state-of-the-art' throughout much of their career. Some airframes are currently being refurbished and reissued to Tactical Air Command as F-111Gs

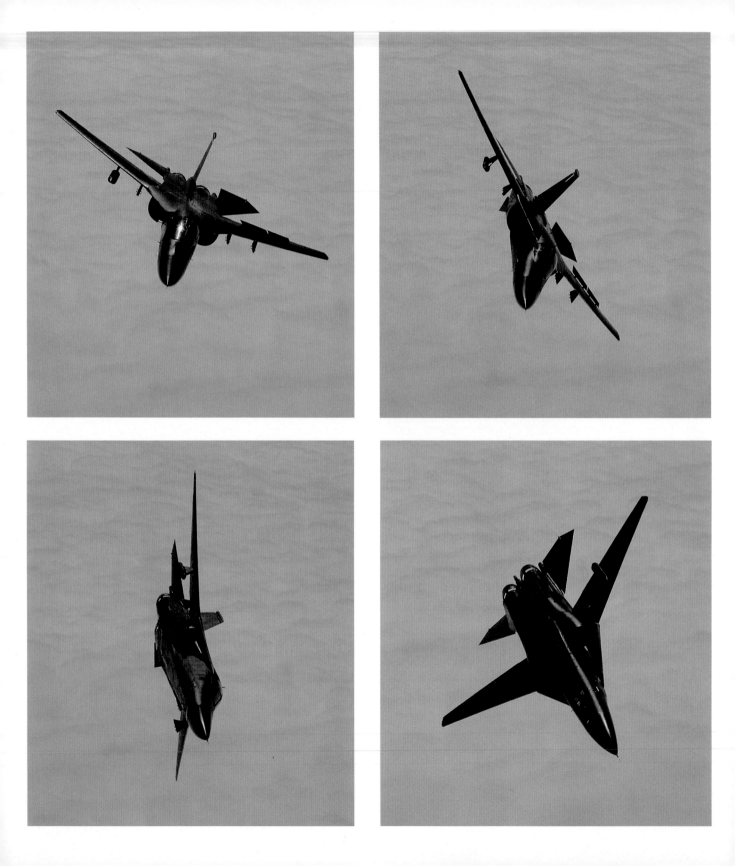

Above The large wing area of the Lockheed TR-1 is necessary for high-altitude flight, but inconvenient for landing. As a mission ends at RAF Sculthorpe, a Ford Mustang races down the runway, its driver radioing instructions to the pilot for the final few feet of ground effect

Right 17th Reconnaissance Wing ground crews assist a TR-1A's pilot following a mission. Markings on the red engine intake covers (hanging from the access stand) and on the tail would normally identify this aircraft as serial number 80-1078 – normally, that is, if U-2s and TR-1s were not re-marked for security purposes

'Ghost Rider' (serial 64-14844) is one of eight RC-135Vs assigned to the 55th Strategic Reconnaissance Wing's 38th and 343rd SRSs. Based at Offutt AFB, Nebraska, the aircraft carry special equipment for eavesdropping on electronic transmissions. The fleet of RC-135Vs were converted from seven RC-135Cs and a single RC-135U, making the Victor model the most common of all dedicated reconnaissance variants. Although many sources have stated that the prominent cheek fairings contain side-looking airborne radar (SLAR), this is far from the truth. A variety of other sensors are fitted in these fairings instead

Penn Guard

Air National Guard units are assigned through inter-state and intra-state command structures. The four National Guard aircraft in this series of photos are assigned to the governor of Pennsylvania; through the USAF they follow different chains of command. The EC-130 of the 193rd Special Operations Group (SOG) (Harrisburg) reports directly to AFSOC; the KC-135E of the 171st ARefw (Pittsburgh) reports to SAC (with subordinate units assigned to Rickenbacker ANGB, Ohio, and McGuire AFB, New Jersey); the A-7D of the 112th TFG (also Pittsburgh) reports to TAC's 9th AF through the 127th TFW at Selfridge ANGB, Michigan; and the OA-10A of the 111th TASG (Willow Grove) reports to TAC's 12th AF through the 128th TFW at Truax, Wisconsin

Below Representatives of the Pennsylvania Air National Guard assembled in late summer 1991; prior to this formation, the four flying units had never shared the same air space

Left The camera-ship (a two-seat A-7K from the 112th TFG) switches sides, providing this unusually intimate view of a *Volant Solo* EC-130. Note the large cooling position tucked beneath the wing root

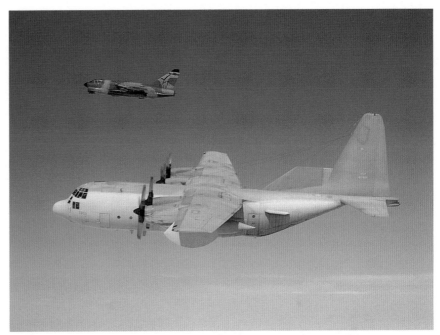

Above 'Steel 11' rides off 'Baton 01's' right wing. Fully designated EC-130E(RR)s, the eight highly modified Hercules were deployed to the Gulf for classified *Volant Solo* sorties over enemy lines, the aircraft's psychological warfare and communications intelligence gathering equipment being used in a campaign to urge Iraqi soldiers to surrender

Left When fully kitted out in *Volant Solo* configuration, the EC-130 has a higher operational weight (empty) than any other C-130 in service with the USAF. Some of the obvious external changes include prominent blade antennae affixed outboard of the engines and on the spine of the aircraft, heat exchangers on either side of the fuselage just forward of the cargo door, and wingtip and tail pods for trailing wire antennae

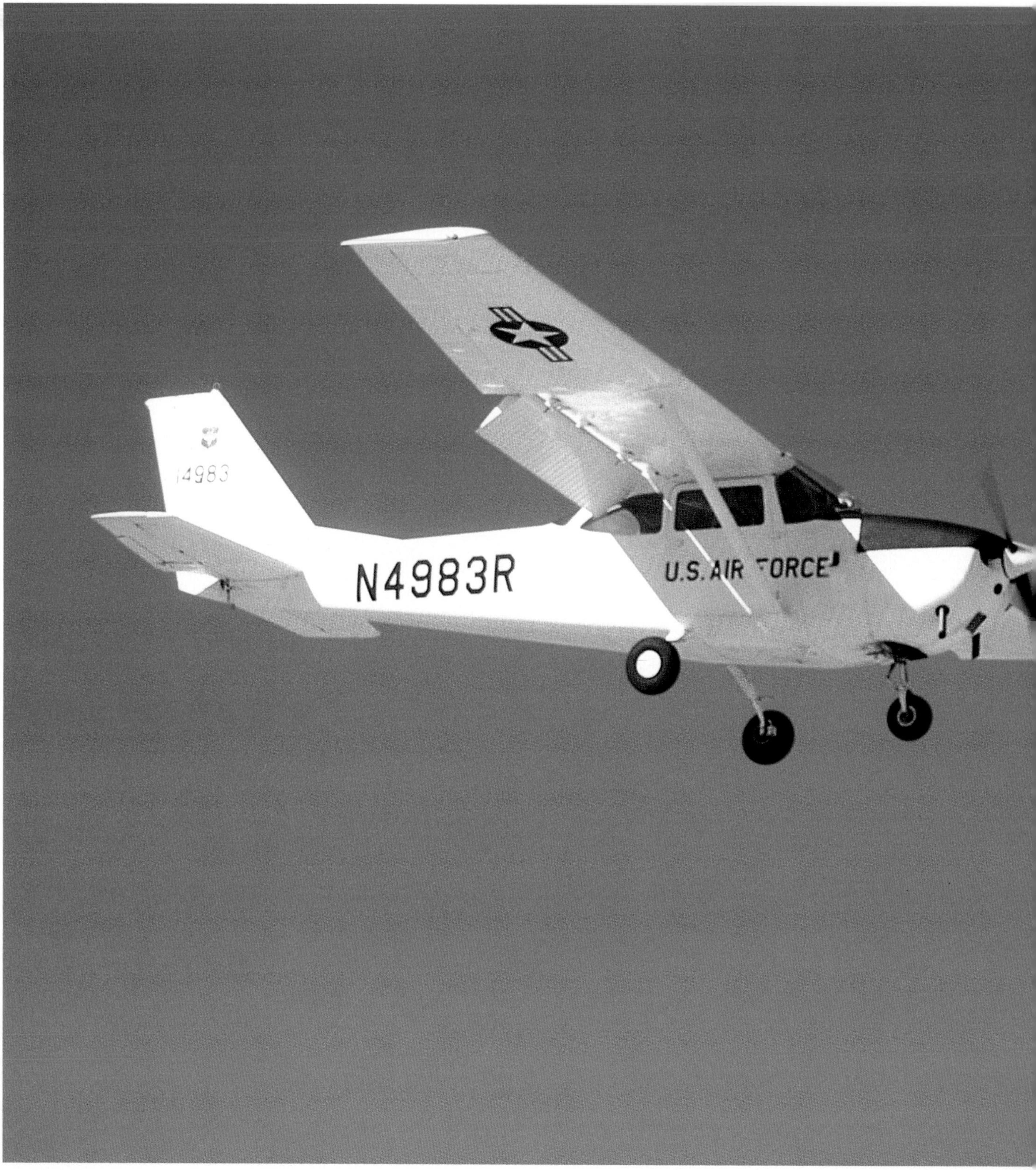
14983
N4983R
U.S. AIR FORCE

Training Command

Air Training Command (ATC) recruits, trains, and commissions the men and women of the US Air Force. This mission includes the undergraduate training of pilots (through six flying training wings), navigators (through the 323rd Flying Training Wing), and instructor pilots (through the 12th Flying Training Wing).

Left Students who have not received primary flight training through Reserve Officers Training Corps (ROTC) or the Air Force Academy begin with the 1st FSS (Flight Screening Squadron) at Hondo Field, Texas. Assigned to the 12th FTW, the 1st FSS provides eight hours of classroom instruction and eleven flights in T-41As during a sixteen-day programme

Below T-41s are military versions of the Cessna 172. Note the US civil registrations, which are based on the military serial numbers

Above Based at Randolph AFB, Texas, the 12th FTW takes qualified military pilots and trains them to become instructor pilots. Cessna T-37 Tweets are assigned to the 559th FTS

Left The standard colour scheme for T-37s employs insignia white upper surfaces and insignia blue undersurfaces. Tweets assigned to Randolph do not carry any form of unit identification markings

Above Although not considered a high performance aircraft, the T-37 is surprisingly agile, its twin Continental J69-T-25 turbojets giving the Cessna a modicum of fighter-type performance

Right '. . . and touched the face of God.' A backdrop of cumulus towers above a 12th FTW T-37

Above The flight leader drops through a traditional Texas summer rainstorm just as he cycles through the gear extension prior to lining up to the runway

Left A slick formation of four T-37s over their own flight line at Randolph. As can be seen the base covers a fair slab of Texas, myriad runways criss-crossing the flat dry plains

Above Currently, all pilots who complete T-37 training move up to the T-38 Talon, a supersonic advanced trainer. In 1992 ATC will tailor advanced training, reserving the T-38 for bomber and fighter pilots and moving tanker and transport pilots to the new T-1A Jayhawk (based on the Beech 400 civil executive transport)

Left Gear down and locked, the flight descends towards base. With its wide spread undercarriage, the T-37's landing characteristics are perfectly capable of coping with a typical student's flying skills

Above The Talon's modern lines belie its origins in the 1950s. The hot trainer for generations of pilots, the T-38 should remain in service until 2010

Right A low-altitude echelon formation. Randolph's T-38s, all assigned to the 560th FTS, are marked with white stars on a blue tail band. All ATC T-38s are painted white, following abandonment of an experimental blue-and-white scheme resembling that worn by T-37s

Above and overleaf One by one, two T-38s bank and break away from the rest of the formation

Left The Talon's 25 ft wingspan allows for an unusually close formation. Talons had equipped the Thunderbirds from 1974 until replaced by F-16s in 1983

Above The formation breaks for final approach

Left Finger-four formation over Randolph. The base was built as a training establishment during the early 1930s; the tall building (actually a water tower) at the head of the traffic circle is known as the Taj Mahal

VIPs and SAR

Left Based at Andrews AFB, Maryland, the 1st Helicopter Squadron (HS) flies UN-1Ns in support of headquarters missions for the Air Force District of Washington

Below The 1st HS is assigned to the 89th Airlift Wing. The Insignia Blue and White colour scheme, complete with black and gold trim, is unique to the squadron

Above One of the 102nd's Jolly Greens turns into the morning skies for a practice mission. These veterans of the Vietnam conflict have now been retired to the Davis-Monthan boneyard having completed their service lives after 25 years

Left The 102nd Air Rescue Squadron, Suffolk County, New York, is listed as the Air National Guard's oldest squadron. During the 1980s the unit was equipped with HH-3s and HC-130s

Practising for rapid recovery of pararescuemen, an H-3 drops into a pre-arranged clearing. No fewer than 31 Jolly Greens were lost to enemy action during the Vietnam War as the helicopters were heavily involved in 'Sandy' rescue missions

Above left A second 102nd HH-3 flies over the salt marshes of suburban Long Island

Left During 1991 the 102nd converted to new MH-60 Nighthawks. Flying down the Hudson River, one of the new Nighthawks is a modest presence against the New York skyline

Above A 102nd ARS MH-60 lifts off at Stewart Air National Guard Base as Marine Reserve KC-130s fly above

Heavy Haulers

Five aircraft bear the majority of the USAF's airlift burden. Called 'trash haulers' by fighter jocks (derisively) and airlift crews (honourably), the C-130, C-141, and C-5 are supported on deployment by the cargo-carrying capacity of KC-10 and KC-135 tankers.

Left In an exercise that aircrews describe as 'swappin' spit', two 4th Wing KC-10 practise refuelling each other

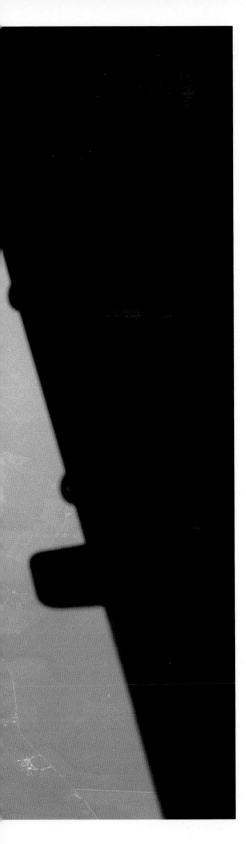

Above and overleaf Refuelling completed, *Mystic Warrior* drops away and moves up alongside 'Regal 21'. Note the Wright Flyer painted on the tail, a marking first worn when the two squadrons were assigned to the 68th ARW

Left *Mystic Warrior* took radio call 'Raven 22' for the mission. It is seen here from the boomer's position of 'Regal 21'

Above Creative camouflaging of the vertical tail has been a subtle trademark of the C-130 since the late 1960s. The aircraft received by the 166th TAG, Delaware ANG, have a grey stylized kangaroo on the right side of each aircraft

Above CDS – the containerized delivery system – allows C-130s to airdrop eight pallets in a relatively small drop zone

Right The photographer's C-130 moves in behind the lead aircraft for this shot from the navigator's astrodome

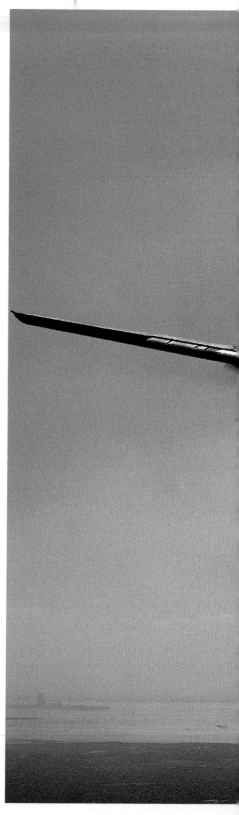

Above South of Wilmington the formation approaches the Delaware Memorial Bridge and some of Delaware's chemical plants and refineries. In the centre background of the photo is the highest point in the state, though at 448 ft above sea level the rise is no landmark!

Right Different aircraft, different topography. The 914th TAG/328th TAS, is based at Niagara Falls, New York. One of the 914th's C-130Es banks as the late afternoon sun casts long shadows

Above The C-141 has provided heavy airlift support to US forces for over 35 years. During the late 1970s and early '80s, the entire fleet was modified to C-141B specs. The modification process strengthened the wing, lengthened the fuselage, and added an aerial refuelling receptacle above the cockpit

Left C-141Bs of the 438th MAW at McGuire AFB, New Jersey. Consistent with the international nature of their missions, most C-141s display US flags on the tail. 438th C-141 is crewed by an associate reserve crew, the AFRES associate programme providing regular Air Force units with additional personnel for all mission duties

Above Heading into the New Jersey sunset, a C-141 closes on McGuire as yet another Atlantic supply mission nears completion. In the course of the year the 438th MAW will make hundreds of crossings to USAFE bases carrying anything from engines to envelopes.

Right The 105th MAG, based at Stewart ANGB, New York, is the only ANG unit assigned C-5 Galaxies. Unit aircraft carry the title 'Empire State' (aka: New York) on the forward fuselage. In this view no fewer than five of the unit's eleven C-5 can be seen ranged up on the Stewart ramp